Adil Dad was born and raised in England. He started his first book PICK ME UP as a passion project but soon discovered an increased passion for writing.

D1452608

RISE is his second book.

rise

a collection of
letters and poems
designed to unite

ADIL DAD

for us.

once we pick ourselves up, we'll try to rise. we'll try to rise but fail, we'll learn that not only does it take hard work to rise but it takes each other, a team. a unifying body of work allowing us all to rise above our previous endeavours.

we may pick ourselves up but together we shall rise.

RISE

YEARNING

REVERIES

HOPE

UNISON

introduction

Is it cliché for me to start by saying "I sit here in a cafe"? But I do, and cafés have become somewhat a second home to me and my writing. I enjoy sitting and watching people go by, while my mind wonders away and ideas appear in my head; ideas of what to write about, ideas of how to express a certain concept so that others may or may not understand. So that others may agree or disagree either way my job is done, I have expressed.

The beauty of life is that we all see it differently, how crazy is that? The same thing is interpreted 7 billion different ways. I experience a sip of coffee differently to how my loved ones do, yet we enjoy it all the same. I sit here writing poetry, ready to be interpreted by a number of different people, we may all have billions of experiences in life but in the end we all feel the same things. This fact in itself inspires me to write, the fact that you can take it your own way, it means something else to you, it becomes your own. This book, right here, right now, it's yours. And I'm beyond grateful to have had an opportunity to write something like this, to produce a body of work like this has been extremely liberating, I'm grateful that this book is in your hand right now, in this moment. I didn't write this book for one particular group of people, I aim for my work to be universal, so that we all can resonate together in something and throughout this book I try my hardest to express themes of unity, compassion, and empathy. Despite it all we don't win this thing of life alone, we win it together.

Throughout this book you'll find poems & short letters. I wouldn't say they're meant to be read in one sitting, I'm hoping its something you can pick up when the feeling arises but if you wish to read it in one sitting that's fine by me.

Poems are very special to me, they're a way of presenting a whole idea in under 100 words, you can express a feeling and you can turn stomachs upside down in less than a minute. Each time I apply pen to paper I'm reminded how truly powerful words are. I started reading poetry in 2013, the poet *Jalaluddin Rumi* has been the biggest influence to my writing. He presents such etiquette in his work, a master of the art. May God bless him. He helped pioneer a passion for writing I never thought I could achieve. He allowed me to see the power poetry holds, the immense positivity and hope you can insert inside of a poem. The amount of lessons it contains to the amount of value, all of this combined was something which was pivotal to my poetry campaign. The letters within this book are addressed to us, my letters are loosely based on the wellness of the human mind and soul. The letters are carefully crafted to present an idea and I hope the ideas have come through as well as I've hoped. I've always kept my non-fiction work online but now I'm exporting to a print format. The idea of my non-fiction work as something tangible was very appealing to me.

Don't be afraid to use the white space for your own thoughts, you may want to write down what a certain poem means to you, this makes it great for when you look back on them.

This whole book has been 2x as challenging as my first. And I truly hope this book adds value to the whole world. The earliest advice I was given regarding publishing a book was "write a book you'd want to read". And here I am, writing a book I'd want to read.

So, shall we begin?

each adventure must
challenge you as much
as your last.

chapter one

RISE

THE RISE

like autumn we fall,
but like spring we
shall rise again.

a circle of
falling and rising.

after each fall the tree grows
taller, wiser and becomes
accustomed to the fall.

familiar with it.
friends with it.

DROWNING

pain is like drowning,
except we don't die.

we survive.
we adapt.
we rise.

FIGHT FOR IT

some days you're west
some days you're so far east.

but remember everyday
that the world needs you.

you possess the
will and might
to do what others
can not dream of.

we need you,
i need you.

because when you find
the chemical balance
the world will not know
what it is in for.

SENSES

once you know that
Love is all you need.

watch how you eat, speak and see.

all of it, in divine moderation.

each sense begins
to fulfil your need to love.

each sense mindful
of its past action.

THE KEY

the key has been around
our necks the whole time.

yet we often look for
people to unlock us.

while we haven't
even unlocked ourselves.

FOUNDATIONS

keep your foundations solid,
feed the pillars and watch your
legacy last a millennia.

the fruits you
nurture will carry
your name forward.

the colour of your
flag will never fade.

THE BRUSH

give.

wherever you are
and whatever state you're in.

for it is the brush that
cleanses the heart.

give in the Givers way,
or give to the creation.

the perfect man gave,
even when he had nothing.

THE MIRROR

we're all mirrors what
i see in you also resides in me.

our reflection will incite
growth, so let us face
each other and grow.

together,
as one.

THE QUESTION

do i truly trust in Him,
or do i just sing the song?

trust requires work.
late nights, early mornings.

give your soul in for reshaping.

once it returns it will be
ready to withstand all seasons,
all calamities and all forces.

no more questioning, only work.

DESIGN

know that we share the
same design principles
as the mountains above us.

no blemish on your
known skin is there
without its purpose.

no molecule on this
earth is without reason.

the reason of our
existence is to sing.

YOUR CANDLE

let your candle shine,
allow it to illuminate others.

and it will illuminate a path for you.

BOUNTIES

patience is the gift that
will never stop pouring.

it pours even when
we have nothing.

it's an endless fountain
waiting for you to
feed on its bounties.

A CHANCE

suffer for the right cause
and status will be elevated.

sacrifice for the omniscient
and await the river of milk.

give what you don't
need for a chance to take
what you deserve.

PHOENIX

being out of your
comfort zone is like
rubbing a block of concrete
against your own skin.

rub a little longer
and await ignition.

soon you'll fly.

higher and brighter
than before.

FLY

spread your wings,
create the balance.

as one rises,
stretch the other
to maintain balance.

do one, without
forgetting about the other.

SOLITUDE

own your solitude
this is where you will grow.

turn off the lights to let
in the true Light.

own it.

guard it from the
lower self, and then turn off the
lights everywhere you go.

BEGGAR

true love is being
granted the ability
to breathe the morning air
while staying forgetful.

so which of His
favours can we deny?

LISTEN

hear the birds sing
in the morning,
be attentive to it all.

listen to the waves as
they tell their story.

listen to the captain of
the ship as he teaches.

we all need a captain
but must all face
the waves alone.

PORTAL

the portal to eternal love
opens every morning.

search for it.

don't allow the sun
to rise without finding it.

for it surely is better
than the sleep.

rise, before the sun.

CHANGE

art changes law,
art changes lives.

we're artists,
so let's paint
a brighter future.

A LETTER TO MYSELF

impatience can turn
to ungrateful very quickly.

tread softly.

everyday since you were
born, has food not made its
way onto your plate?

has a roof not
sheltered you from
what lies outside?

no one has forgotten
you, but yourself.

THE TRUTH

some days we'll walk
towards it other
days we'll crawl.

but we shall never stay
dormant in regards to it.

The Truth finds a way.

but know when we
crawl to it,
it shall run to us.

HUNTERS

go forth and hunt.

be with those
who refill your quiver.

those who
watch your six.

cherish them,
celebrate them.

keep them close.

THE TRUE BOOK

it sits there weathering away,
whilst i close my ears from it.

its a lover seeking attention
but i keep it away from sight.

it sits on the highest shelf,
whilst my heart
resides on the lowest.

HOME

haven't all of the experiences,
the lessons done one thing.

they've all brought
us closer to home.

closer to Him.

SELF

i was once selfish to
chase the fruits of this world.

soon they became tasteless,
Love had done His work.

soon i realised a different
type of selfish, a longing
for the fruits of the next world.

You taught me that
to have all the fruits of the
next world meant giving away
all the fruits of this world.

help me give.

slow

Everything is moving super fast, I'm struggling to grasp it. Nothing is savoured, I feel like I'm just drifting through. Its an outer body experience where I can see myself completing the days as though they're groceries on a shopping list. It's all just passing me by...

The world moves at breakneck speed, everything seems as though its moving twice as fast; the time it takes to receive a message from someone is instant, all they have to do is type it on a device. A vast amount of information is being transferred all at once, we try our best to consume as much as we can.

Stop.

Take that sip of coffee steadily; think about where it came from, think about how many people it took to get to your cup. From farm to barista, that's a lot of people. All so you could enjoy it in peace. We're either living with our future mind or our past mind, never with our today mind. We're either worrying about something that has happened or worrying about what may happen, all of it, most likely to be a micro issue. We're full of thoughts.

Watch life flow in front of you, do not wait for life to flow. Its flowing right now, but are we looking? Sit calm for a few moments, allow yourself to breathe - allow your soul to breathe.

Your thoughts may seem plethoric but if you just breathe, you'll come to the realisation that you are not your thoughts. You are something else entirely. Focussing on the now can, at first, be a difficult task to accomplish. It may take some time to master. Remember that you are exactly where you need to be, if you're constantly waiting for something to happen, it most likely won't happen. We have to accept what position we're in and make a move to change that.

Living in the now can allow you to get things done uncondensed. Single tasking is a great way to access the now, by completing each task with your full attention and with your full effort will present incredible change in the long run. You can achieve 50 things within a day but at what percentage? 50%? Maybe 60%? But when we do less things we have the ability to do said tasks at 70%+. I was introduced to the 80/20 rule by *Timothy Ferriss* in the *4-Hour Work Week*. Its a great rule to determine what to single task on and what to leave out. Out of the 100% of things you do, what 20% of them tasks give you 80% of your overall outcome. After noting down what those are we can proceed. A schedule shouldn't be fully booked, it needs spaces to breathe. A lesson learnt earlier on allowed me to understand that being fully booked all the time sprouts the essence of laziness. Why? Because we may end up neglecting our loved ones, but more importantly ourselves.

Meditation is the shortcut to winning; to have the ability to stop and breathe. To focus on what matters the most. To have a chance to accept what is and what can be, and to have the potential to be grateful is the perfect way to start any day. I remember being super cynical regarding meditation in my early stages; I expected things to happen instantly.

meditates for 5 minutes

"But, I still feel the same"

Meditation is something which has long-term effects - its a ritual, when done correctly, can give us control in any and every situation. For, breathing is the door to all emotional states. When we're anxious our breathing changes, when we're joyful it also changes. To be a master of your breathing is the key to mastering our emotional states.

Moving slow doesn't happen overnight, it will always be a transition. It will take time and practice, just remember to keep breathing now and then.

past

present

future

now matters.
not yesterday.
not tomorrow.

chapter two

YEARNING

TRUST

trust will mend all
the pieces together.

without it, everything
becomes ruptured.

trust will mend us all.

so allow me to trust.
for at times i dip
knowing i shouldn't.

THE RETURN

in our nature,
we're such micro beings.

yet sometimes we feel like
we've been beyond this universe.

we all feel it,
i've asked.

we've been to a
place we can't picture.
seen things we can't comprehend.

this is what we
all long for.

to return.

NIRVANA

that night you once felt
that specific way,
search for it again.

put away your
black mirror.

and look carefully,
search beyond the black holes.

beyond the known universe,
search inside you.

that is where it lies.

THE FIRST

your first Love.

the one that matters,
if the connection needs
to be re-established then re-establish.

witness this love change
your actions your view, your words.

YOU SEE IT

know that your world-view
needn't be accepted by others.

only by yourself.

you see the atoms of
the waves different to others.

you see the salt
inside the sea.

you also see the green.
and it makes you, you.

PERSISTENCE

sometimes you may
feel like giving up.

some of us even may.

but the beauty is
in the struggle.

the persistence to keep
each single cell fighting.

that's something.

SHAPE

the more i learn
the more i realise
i know nothing.

i wish to go fast
to consume it all.

excessive consumption
will only get me so far.

if my soul isn't in shape
it can't handle the waves.

ARMOUR

allow Trust to be your shield
and even the wisest of kings
wont be able to bring you down.

let the army of
thousands march forth.

for this is an armour
no man can pierce.

BLUEPRINT

a young man approaches a
crowded souk and notices a stranger
crying he asks the stranger, "why do you cry?"

the stranger replies, "we've won; we're winners,
we have the prayers of the perfect man."

he then asks the stranger, "explain!"

the stranger sits him down and replies, "the blueprint
so perfect, each detail has been thought out, down to
the atom. we have it all. the book breathes light, so
why do we inhale the darkness?"

LET GO

let go.
oh brother, oh sister.
let go.

cut the strings that
dangle from your neck.

be free from it all
allow for another form
of subjugation the
subjugation of yourself.

take back control,
control of the soul.

TO YOU

i did it again,
i tried running before walking.

i stumbled again.

teach me to run,
so i may run to You.

A FIRE

when the stomach turns
inside out and the fire starts.

turn to Him, for He is home
and we are homesick.

FIND ME

You sent the perfect
man, the brightest of them all.

the light of the universe.
the guiding light. the highest light.

today we measure in lumens
but i'm certain he would
break its known barrier.

he is the light, while i
bathe in the darkness.

the universe would not
shine without him.

oh, best of mankind
share your light.

for if i'm to be in
jeopardy on the that day.

find me.
find us all.

WHITE SHORES

let my passion for him
increase, allow my every action
to be influenced by his.

and if my love for him
ever drops, i've lost.

i become of no use.
for he is the key.

the key to the white shores.

SEARCHING

we may spend years
chasing what we want.

while what we need
finds us without us knowing.

its under our nose,
while we search
beyond the stars.

its inside us, while
we're busy looking outside.

THE GATE OF LIGHT

for when we smile we
open the gate of light.

so smile and share
a piece of your soul.

so smile and shine
your light onto the world.

WE RISE

his way is a well
amidst a dry desert.

life within a lifeless galaxy.

through perfection You guided me.

the perfect blueprint, not only
for me but for the
whole of mankind.

so that together we rise.

THE RIVER

we have been taught by
perfection how to put
out fires in hearts.

to build rivers inside,
rivers that flow through.

so each time a fire
would start, the river assists.

PEACE CAME FROM YOU

how do i explain
what happens?

when i sing your praise
each ounce of despair slowly
disappears from my
body into the abyss.

each atom of darkness,
replaces with light.

PASSIVE

my light.
my guide.

you have shown me
the perfect way but i lack
the power to walk it.

i'm passive,
without strength.

ignorant and without light.

THE GARDENS

friends of mine,
let us walk into
the gardens.

meet me there, amongst
the never ending fields.

if my soul isn't
there, find me.

BEARERS

the diamonds will
always consume.

you can convince
yourself they wont.

ask the bearer,
he went to destroy them,
but they consumed him.

he fell, while claiming
them his own.

none of this is ours.

we're only vessels bearing
these riches till its our time.

own less, be more

To my delight it arrived, the new one. The packaging was pure white and crisp. The smell of fresh metal was brisk to the nose. I peeled off the plastic and was met with a face in ecstasy reflecting off the black mirror before me. "Oh, you've got the new one" they said, I replied with a smile. Each time it made its way out of my pocket, my pride filled eyes would smile. But it wasn't long before they themselves announced 'a new one'. And within seconds, my new one became old. And within milliseconds, that reflection of ecstasy turned into misery.

If I told you that tomorrow you were going on a trip to a different country; if I asked you to pack only what you needed, ask yourself, what you would pack? Would you pack all your shirts or just the three that you need? Would you pack several shoes or just one pair of comfortable shoes which weigh the least and allow you to travel light. If I was to answer this question a few years ago, I would've told you that I needed a bigger bag.

I once remember owning at least every coloured shirt, every type of trouser and most types of shoes. I remember wanting to own the latest and be known for it. Somehow, somewhere I had been wired to think that having materials defined who I was, as a person. I had been taught that owning plentiful would make me happy. The world is designed to make us feel like we're being left in the past if we don't own the latest. But it turns out that, we don't need to have the latest to be happy. This consumer culture had trapped me. Trapped me from attaining a freedom I was looking for.

I came to a halt. I took a birds-eye view of all that I had consumed. I remember asking myself about what truly matters, in terms of objects. The materials we own are tools, they're designed for function, to serve a purpose in our lives. The minute we turn their functions into anything other than that, is where the danger lies. The instant we amount love for these materials is where greed may consume us.

Thus began my journey; the journey of owning less, the journey of being more. I kept asking one question for each item: does this add value to me? Can I live without this? For clothes, it was a matter of knowing how often I'd wear the garment throughout the year. If I wouldn't wear it as much as my other pieces, I'd purge. And after purging around 70% of my items I began to feel it. A feeling of liberation, a different type of weight being lifted off my shoulders. This connection I had to my things wasn't just a physical one, it was a cerebral one too.

Soon, this ritual I carried out into my physical life began to manifest in my mental life. I became a lot more conscious of the clutter in my mind. What thoughts / baggage did I keep in there? I began to remove the noise and focussed on only things that I gained value from.

A benefit I gained from this was the reclamation of time; I wasn't engaged in mindless activities, rather in the stuff I truly enjoyed. I began to discover a true, intense passion for things that were only half explored previously. I was going all in on things, relationships, work, and health.

The material possessions I owned were obstructing my personal / spiritual growth. I allowed them to have way too much meaning in my life. But the more I detached, the more I became unshackled. I started to make more conscious buying decisions. Before tapping the card reader, I asked, do I really need this? And the underlying truth is that we don't really need about 90% of the items that are on sale today.

Once the excess is removed, as humans we only need loving relationships, meaningful work and good health. The things we simply can't function without. These things are pinnacle to our soul - and pinnacle to our happiness.

things we don't need:

- a huge house
- enormous wealth
- designer clothes
- a stylish car
- a powerful job

things we need:

- time
- meaningful work
- great health
- good books
- loving relationships

materials don't deserve
a place in our hearts,
people do.

chapter three

REVERIES

REVERIE

i wish for your radiance
to appear in my sleep.

but i wish for it, only once
my vessels are pure.

pure for your presence.

i am not deserving
of your gaze, but oh
how my soul craves it.

i hear it crying at
times of despair.

and when the path
seems unclear, when the
darkness covers all, your
name lights the way.

BLIND

i was blind to try and
quench my thirst from
the cup of this world.

when there lay an
ocean inside of me.

OPPOSITES

they urged me to
wear the shirts of gold.

while He provided
a cape of righteousness.

they taught me to
fear the liars.

while He taught
me to fear nothing.

DIVINE BLEMISH

a blemish can humble
even the most
arrogant of men.

never ask why the sand
contains pebbles but
know that we were wired
by The Master Tactician.

WISE MEN

the wise man wakes
to feed his soul.

trusting that Love
will provide for his body.

forgive me,
for i have been unwise.

CITY OF LIGHT

allow me to rest among
the soil of light, within
the city of Light.

let my tears blend
with the blessed soil.

let my soul sing
the song of Love.

then let me sleep forever,
within the city of Light.

INTERNAL PAIN

it hurts inside
we've all felt it.

but answer my question,
is it pain or is it the
calling from beyond?

so when we feel it together,
we may sing the song,
together.

NO MORE

no more must we
conform to their ideals.

no more will we
follow their ways.

no more will we
buy into their ads.

no more will we be
fooled by insecurities
they said we have.

no more shall we be
formed into play
things they can play with.

COMPANION

im the shield while
she's the sword,
dagger and arrow.

i take siege while she
fiercely attacks.

i take siege while she
strikes down the enemy.

A LONELY CRAFT

how do you get good?
you become obsessed.

how do you become obsessed?
you learn everything about it.

how?
by loving it.

how do you love it?
by loving yourself.

FORM

you will burn
brightest, but only
when you're ready.

so take siege.

the milky way will
watch in awe,
as you light up half
of the universe.

BOOKS

we're all open books,
but know that not everyone
has the ability to read.

some just enjoy turning pages.

THE JOURNEY

your journey calls to you,
are you listening?

its ready to take you to places
beyond your imagination.

pack your bag,
but leave your diamonds.

for what you return with
will be something my writing
prowess can't describe.

FEED

before you feed
others fill your
cup first.

let it overflow
let it be untamed.

then, feed them.

the digital age

Read 18:23

The connection has been made, but still something feels missing. Each time, I wonder what's missing from this connection. Perhaps its the fact that only half of a connection has been received, visually through the eyes and stimulation through the mind. The brain has been touched while the soul has been neglected. A half-assed connection.

We live in an age where 80% of the things we interact with is automated; pre-programmed by a machine to predict an outcome. Fuelled by our consumption habits, this algorithm adapts to keep up, to learn what we do, and how we do it. Attracting us to the certain app / program for longer. Designed to make us feel rewarded each time we get a new like, follow or subscribe. We're then subconsciously looking out for this reward each time we upload something. Uploading to the internet isn't a bad thing, but what tends to form is an addiction, and as I'm sure we've all learnt, too much of anything will make you sick.

Have you ever found yourself scrolling for around 5 minutes on a certain app? This is called a dopamine loop. The brain seeks instant pleasure, and this instant pleasure becomes addicting; it's even a known fact that certain companies hire engineers to specifically tailor apps in order for it to be an addiction. The more time we spend on these apps, the more valuable these apps become. Valuable to who? To advertisers. Advertisers seek attention; people to look at their ads, and currently the place where the most attention is, happens to be the internet. Ever notice how mentally exhausted you feel after scrolling for so long? Well, that's because your attention is on sale. You are on sale, to the highest bidder. Each ad has been placed there by design. Research suggests that by spending a day online, we can run into 2500 ads. Now, advertisers buying attention isn't something new, it has been around for some time, but the way it's changed today is the fact that there is now 10x more data for these advertisers to reach, our interests, our likes / dislikes. This ranges from where we like to eat to what clothes we wear. All of it, for sale.

Detaching from the smartphone was the wisest decision I made in 2017. It allowed me to use the internet less, and to be more mindful whenever I was logged onto the internet. What was my time spent on? To unplug from all the noise, to say good-bye to all the re-targeted ads was liberating. No human should be auctioned for. It allowed me to be 3x as productive as I previously was. Too much noise can have a negative subconscious influence on you. If you ever feel annoyed as to why you haven't been as productive within a certain day, don't be. It's not your fault; the app has been designed that way. However, what you can do to fix it, is limit your time; be mindful of how much time you use on these digital devices and what on. Are you writing your papers, or binging the latest season of *Stranger Things*? Devices have somehow become the primary: whenever we need to check something of importance, we ask the computer first, instead of the knowledgeable people. Whenever we need directions, it's almost criminal to approach a stranger.

After replying to messages through my laptop, I started to realise how unfulfilling it was. Talking to another human via social apps was not beneficial. When we're engaged in a direct message, conversation through these social apps rarely tends to last long; once the dopamine hit has been received, the conversation becomes rid of its value, hence it no longer provides what it once did. It becomes purged of air. Our deepest conversations have dissolved into pixels, emotions strayed. When we talk to someone face-to-face the body language, the eye contact, the subtle mannerisms, all of it intact, all of the stuff that makes us human, who we truly are, is there.

a unproductive morning:

- email
- facebook
- messages
- instagram
- youtube

a productive morning:

- meditation
- work-out
- reading
- breakfast
- journalling

danger lies, whenever
we exceed moderation.

chapter four

HOPE

KNOWLEDGE

so, you want to know the
secrets of the world.

then learn about yourself.

learn about the universe
that resides in you.

only then does knowledge
become second nature.

UNISON

ever notice how beautiful
it feels when you witness a group
of people singing in conjunction?

this is unity.

our souls singing,
craving to be one.

UNDERESTIMATION

don't settle for puddles when
you can own entire oceans.

THE WAR

in order to rise above our
demons we must apply discipline.

with our armour by our side,
we must attend the war, wholly.

CHISEL

pain is the chisel
of the soul.

hammer away to become
your ultimate form.

never stop, only settle
for a masterpiece.

THE WAY HOME

ready the runway today,
so that tomorrow we may fly.

attend the call,
and be seated.

for the captains
know the way.

BELONGING

give financially.
give physically.
give mentally.

give everything tangible,
apart from your soul.
that belongs elsewhere.

JEWELS

the times are tough
and maybe you ask for the jewels.

are your pockets large enough?

surely, jewels corrupt
under bad supervision.

MY PATH

where do i come from?
why do they tell me to go this way?
or that way?

i'm confused.

what's the answer?
which way is correct?

i'm just floating in this vessel,
while a thousand voices guide me.

shush. i tell them.

this path is mine.

i shall eat the fruits
i intend to grow.

HOPE

i hope my soul is clean
when i meet You.

i hope it makes
it past the bridge.

above all,
i hope You're pleased.
with it.

A LESSON

she taught me it all.

everything i know, from how to love
the littlest of creatures, to dealing
with the mightiest of calamities.

she taught me that there
is beauty in all of it. the good, the bad,
and the unbearable.

she taught me that
love finds love, so love.

THE DOOR

i entered multiple times,
i showed myself in.

helped myself to fruits
and saw myself out.

and then i wonder
why the fruits
were not sweet.

for the door is always
open. but i rarely sit to talk.

THEIR RACE

they have us racing
against each other.

a never ending paradox.

to one up each other,
to envy a brother.

forfeit.
turn away.
be free.

for this race isn't
made for us.

we just want to be.

WORK

work in your shadow
where no-one can see you.

work till the
shadow is no more.

work till you
become the light.

INFINITY

talk about Infinity and
feel the veils slowly ease
as though the earth stood
still to your specific need.

which of His
favours can we deny?

REJOICE

hard times will bring out patience,
easy times will bring out gratitude.

each time the soul elevates.

praises to You, allow us to
rejoice with the song of Love.

THE CALL

attend the call
of the soul for
it is pure and
full of beauties.

reject the call of
the lower self.

for desires only
lead us into the abyss.

CHEF

never rush,
let it marinate.

the longer it marinates
the sturdier the taste becomes.

you're the chef of
this kitchen so
master your craft.

stay patient, when opening
night is upon you the whole
world will want a taste.

FREEDOM

no grain of sand is
ever misplaced.

you are exactly where
you need to be.

the exact place and time
all of it, calculated.

you've always been free.

SUBMISSION

only when we submit to Him
will we maintain the heart of a lion.

only when we follow
the righteous
will we be raised
with one of them.

THE BELOVED & THE LION

everything i need
to know, taught by them.

i sit blind when they've
taught so many lessons?

who's they?

God's beloved
and His lion.

LIARS

you hide behind your
pocket while inflicting
injustice onto innocence.

you lust for power whilst
feeding off the powerless.

liars are born
into exposure.

soon your disguise
will be eaten by the pack.

so, hell to the liars.

LONGING

longing for things can
increase the more we learn.

the lover longs for her beloved
the more she knows about him.

she learns the patterns
of each atom,
the order beyond the chaos.

the more she knows the
more the longing increases.

so learn.

FEEL

detach from this world
so you feel nothing of it.

attach to the Infinite
and feel His currency.

let it flow through you.

open the bank to allow
the river to flow.

THE LIONESS

in her hospitality the
pack comes first.

she defends the tribe
till her last breath.

she seeks out the
night for shelter.

they will eat first,
while she washes her paws.

YOU

its you.
your taste in things.
your view on life.

that's the difference.
the catalyst.
it's 1 in 7 billion.

so own it.

YOUR NEW EMPIRE

stay silent,
build an empire,
and tell no one.

stay silent,
grow your mind,
and tell no one.

stay silent,
feed your soul,
and tell no one.

THE POWER OF LOVE

when we want something
don't the atoms of this universe
tear through the fabric of reality
just for it to be?

so which of His
favours can we deny?

EQUATION

when it's all said and
done, through all of it
i end up with the same answer.

each time, it calculates to it.
through my sweat, blood and tears
the answer remains the same.

that i can't function without You.

BY CHANCE

nothing,
i am nothing.

let me lay,
lay and release all
that my eyes hold.

what did i do?
i've done nothing.

why me,
why us?

i'm a beggar with
nothing of value
to my name.

yet by Your plan
i'm born into this
community of Light.

ACCESS

the truth reaches so
many hidden depths.
once you find it, submerge.

explore it whole
without missing an atom.

for the truth is access to the infinite.

YOUR PLAN

there is a community of light
in which flowers bloom.

the closer to the light the root is
the stronger the branches become.

there is a community of light
where everyone is accepted.
where no single cell is averted.

there is a community of light
where we all share the same boat.
its where grandeur radiates.

there is a community of light
which we sometimes stray from.

and when the nights are darkest
the community shines and
illuminates the way.

there is a community of light.
there is, but can we see it?

REMOVE AND PROCEED

happiness isn't adding
things to our lives,
its knowing what to take away.

so remove, and just be.

CURRENCY

The man with Love on
his side wins in both worlds.

he becomes both sides of the coin.

underestimation

A Friend: I really want to pursue archery.

Me: As a hobby? Or athlete level?

A Friend: Oh, I'd love to do be an athlete, but I don't think I'd be good enough.

The second we say we can't achieve something is the same second we close the possibility of it ever happening. Whatever we set in our heads will be the outcome. Underestimation is something I'm guilty of too. As humans we tend to do this quite often. Why can't you achieve what you want? There is no difference between us and the person that has already achieved the certain task.

I once spent a while thinking I wasn't good enough to do certain things; I'm sure we all do. I'm here to tell you that its all in your head. The way you see things, you may see the mountain before you, but you may dismiss your wings. This could overwhelm us and restrict us from pursuing our certain dream. But however, I'm here to tell you that the mountain is only as big as you make it. The only thing standing in the way of the mountain is ourselves. Nothing truly controls us; the fluctuation in our progress is down to us. Blame can never be outsourced. You need to remember that this is *your* journey and no one else's. So proceed as you wish, knowing that you must take accountability for your actions. Also know another thing, you are good enough for anything in this life; the second you remove the fear from your heart is when the door opens.

Why do we underestimate ourselves? We may sometimes get trapped focussing on another's progress; we begin to compare journeys. Yes, Dwayne Johnson wakes up at 4AM each day, but focussing on his progress will only halt our own progress. We shouldn't care what level X person is on; if it inspires you, stay inspired, if anything else, look away. Comparison is the biggest poison known to man, it will only halt our own progress. If we're stuck living in someone else's expectation of us, then it leaves us with no room to expand. Know that work must be done, so master your craft. Become great. Others may say things, so we must exist in our own sandbox, free from comments, its existence should incite growth. Growth of craft. Take the leap. Some days it may take risk, some days you'll be so far from your comfort zone, but breathe because this is where you'll thrive.

We all have the ability to become athlete level archers, but how many of us are willing to do what it takes?

In order to do so, we must rise above our ego. We must leave it at the door, along with all the voices and comparisons. Let nothing stand in the way of you and your what you wish to achieve. Know your goals, remind yourself of them each morning. Know how you work, so that you may construct a schedule that fits with your brain schedule.

So, what're you waiting for?

how far we think we can go.

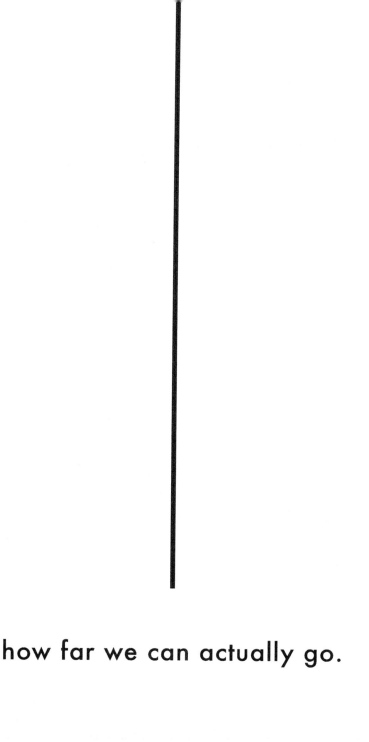

how far we can actually go.

our ego must be locked
away. for if we are to
rise, it must fall.

chapter five

UNISON

THE GIVER

when we want more jewels
we get acquainted with
the jewel giver.

we sway and swift
till he gives.

we bend and break,
till we have
more than enough.

we have now sold
something valuable to
us only to realise
that the giver is temporary.

maybe we had
the right idea.

we were just acquainted
with the wrong giver.

UNLEARN

in order to learn new things,
first we must de-clutter.

we sometimes need
to remove before adding.

rid the ocean of its
blemishes, filter them out.

we must shake the branches
till the weak leaves fall,
so only the strong remain.

then we must add.

YATHRIB

the true value of time
is experienced here.

the sky emits its
own unique shade.

while the air sits
holding a musk i
can't completely describe.

the natives, calm.
the nourishments, plentiful.

the blessings, eternal.

INTERNAL WAR

i found peace while
in a raging war.

it greeted me while
i hid in the trenches.

and together
we signed the treaty.

MERCY

mercy is a muscle
we must nurture,
we must allow it
to consume us.

for Love controls all aspects,
our reach can only go so far.

mercy will bring nations together
and unite the hearts of the world.

for we all crave this,
ever so deeply.

i feel it in the
hearts of people,
as well as my own.

you feel it too.

GREEN

grass can be grown
in most parts of the world.

despite its pigmentation it
will remain as grass.

so remove the veils,
see all types of grass.

then we reign, together.

CALCULATED

perhaps we are lost
in this prison, constantly evolving.

finding several versions of ourselves.

each new version readies
us for what's to come.

leaving what has been,
all of it, in its correct place.

all of it calculated
by The Master Tactician.

do nothing, do nothing but be.

for it has all been written.

ASSETS

put Love before anything and
witness Him put you first.

and like this mountains
will fall at your feet.

the stars become yours,
so that you may win the war.

KNOW

those cards you've
been dealt, know where
they come from.

learn, and then
claim your diamonds.

ENERGIES

the energy we pour
into the universe
ultimately defines our outcome.

be kind, for kindness
will find you in the
most unexpected of places.

be unkind, and despair will
meet you at your doorstep.

CATS & DOGS

we spend years
chasing what we want.

while what we need finds us
without our knowing.

this is the way He loves.

YOUR REACH

aim to fulfil your
potential in this life.

peak all mountains,
touch all stars.

shine your light
on everything.

especially the darkness.

YOUR WORK

your best work is the
work with the
most you in it.

the one in which your
soul exists, within its
pages or pixels, go.

go and spread your light.

THE SEAL

what does he look like?
we cant see him?

we're influenced by his
actions and his words.

with the moon at his command
his actions enlightened the world.

he left the largest mark.
he didn't wear a cape.

he wore a seal.

TRUE IDENTITY

maybe the black
mirrors we own
hold our true nature.

perhaps they show us
who we truly are.

behind closed doors,
infinite access and power.

do we rise above it
or consume it all?

RESTRAINTS

close your eyes,
see with your soul.

for it will lay down beauties
you never knew existed.

close your ears,
listen with your soul.

it will tell you tales
of the unknown.

restrain your tongue,
speak with your soul.

it will speak a language
which emits love.

A SPECIAL LOVE

there is a special love
if you submit to it,
it will continue to give.

there is a special love,
if you don't submit to it,
it will continue to give.

there is a special love,
there is.

LOSSES

sometimes we may lose
but learn things we never
thought our minds could fathom.

this is how He loves.

divine lessons,
in the form of losses.

THE FOUNTAIN

i'll forever be a
student sipping from
the fountain of knowledge.

and when i meet
the soil my only
regret will be why i
didn't drown in the fountain.

PROVISIONS

allow me to reach
ecstasy every night.

you are the giver,
so allow my soul to pour.

give me what i need
so i may rise.

give us what we need
so we may rise.

THE TREE

it is ok.

you are where you need
to be, The Eternal Lover
is looking over you.

know that the tree
sometimes needs
to manoeuvre while growing
in order to be on the correct path.

THE SEARCH

together we are uniform
and together we will search
for the light.

two lovers on the infinite search,
the meeting is imminent.

it's only a matter of time
and a matter of
how patient.

INJUSTICE

they harmed you,
caused injustice.

does it matter?

since when did petty
winds change the
structure of a mountain?

YOURS

your narrative
your picture.

don't you dare think it
doesn't matter.

your potential is what
you think it can reach.

never what others say
you can reach.

there is a painting
which needs to be painted.

so paint it.

BY EXAMPLE

we must clean our palace.

so when others see
a clean palace, it will
influence them to clean theirs.

MY FORM

keep me a beggar so Your
name remains on my tongue.

keep me without my wants
so i return to The One who
governs my needs.

TOMORROW

today you maybe don't
feel like walking but i promise
you, tomorrow you'll fly.

THE GAME PLAN

master your craft,
master the industry.

master your ego,
master the world.

this is our world

our internal state incites a far
darker external state.

you feel it too, don't you?

as a collective our wrongdoings
impact the world we live in.
the fumes rise, while glaciers fall.

you feel it too, don't you?

we all want the same thing,
that's just to be.

you feel it too, don't you?

Imagine a world in which together we grew, a world where we gathered resources, ideas and practices from all the tribes and formed one master system where the best practises were utilised. A world where we learn and grow from each other, one in which we accepted other viewpoints and opinions. One where we recognise each and every colour, as our brothers and sisters. A world where love is the universal language.

The things we do for personal gain need to come to an end for if we are to rise we may have to sacrifice our food for those with no plates. To know that this is a team game simply isn't enough.

We now strive to leave this earth, run away from our problems. Start afresh, a clean slate. Is this truly the answer? All it takes is one. Help one person, look out for one person and that'll start a chain reaction in which we'll inspire that one person to help another. And like this our internal affairs shall reflect externally. We have the potential to put things right, between one another, from soul to soul, from tribe to tribe.

you want us all
to eat together, at one table?

you feel it too, don't you?

you feel it too,
because i do.

for, we are the same.
two mirrors, facing each other.

whatever judgment i make
of you also lies in me.

if i'm to fix myself,
you also fix.

so lets mend each other.

lets mend each other
and then rise.

once we rise,
we reign.

to love a neighbour,
is to love the whole world.

acknowledgement

I'd like to thank my editor Raiyana for correcting my numerous grammar mistakes. I couldn't have done this without you.

Written by Adil
Printed in England

reference

you can use this page to jot down your
favourite page numbers for you to refer back to

other publications:

pick me up

a collection of
poems designed to uplift.

reign

2019

CPSIA information can be obtained
at www.ICGtesting.com
Printed in the USA
BVOW09s2122030518
515186BV00002B/251/P